50 Premium Delicious Bacon Recipes

By: Kelly Johnson

Table of Contents

- Bacon-Wrapped Filet Mignon
- Maple-Glazed Bacon Donuts
- Bacon-Wrapped Scallops
- Candied Bacon Skewers
- Bacon Jam Bruschetta
- Chocolate-Dipped Bacon
- Bacon and Cheddar Stuffed Mushrooms
- Bacon-Wrapped Asparagus Bundles
- Bacon-Wrapped Chicken Bites
- Avocado Bacon Breakfast Toast
- Bacon-Wrapped Pork Tenderloin
- Bacon Mac and Cheese
- Bacon-Wrapped Jalapeño Poppers
- Bacon-Wrapped Shrimp
- Bacon and Egg Breakfast Pizza
- BLT Pasta Salad
- Bacon Cheeseburger Sliders
- Bacon-Wrapped Meatloaf
- Bacon-Wrapped Dates with Goat Cheese
- Cheddar Bacon Biscuits
- Bacon-Wrapped Salmon Fillet
- Brussels Sprouts with Bacon and Garlic
- Bacon-Wrapped Cheese Sticks
- Sweet and Spicy Bacon Crackers
- Carbonara with Crispy Bacon
- Bacon-Wrapped Hot Dogs
- Bacon and Mushroom Risotto
- Bacon and Potato Frittata
- Bacon-Wrapped Pineapple Bites
- Bacon-Wrapped Corn on the Cob
- Bacon-Wrapped Onion Rings
- Bacon-Stuffed Chicken Breast
- Bacon Pancakes with Syrup
- Bacon-Wrapped Sausage Links
- Bacon and Spinach Quiche

- Grilled Bacon-Wrapped Peaches
- Bacon Caesar Salad
- Bacon and Cheddar Deviled Eggs
- Bacon-Wrapped Meatballs
- Bacon-Wrapped Mozzarella Sticks
- Maple-Bacon Ice Cream
- Bacon and Brie Grilled Cheese
- Bacon-Wrapped Avocado Fries
- Bacon Cornbread Muffins
- Sweet Chili Bacon Wings
- Lobster with Bacon Butter
- Bacon-Stuffed French Toast
- Bacon-Wrapped Water Chestnuts
- Bacon and Apple Grilled Sandwich
- Bacon-Wrapped Turkey Breast

Bacon-Wrapped Filet Mignon

Ingredients:

- 4 filet mignon steaks (6–8 oz each)
- 4 slices of thick-cut bacon
- 2 tablespoons olive oil
- 2 garlic cloves, minced
- 1 teaspoon fresh rosemary, finely chopped (optional)
- 1 teaspoon kosher salt
- 1/2 teaspoon black pepper
- 2 tablespoons unsalted butter
- Toothpicks

Instructions:

1. **Preheat the Oven:**
   - Preheat your oven to 400°F (200°C).
2. **Prepare the Steaks:**
   - Pat the filet mignon dry with paper towels.
   - Season both sides generously with salt, pepper, garlic, and rosemary (if using).
3. **Wrap the Steaks in Bacon:**
   - Wrap each filet with a slice of bacon, securing the ends with a toothpick.
4. **Sear the Steaks:**
   - Heat olive oil in an oven-safe skillet over medium-high heat.
   - Once hot, sear the steaks for 1–2 minutes per side until browned.
5. **Transfer to the Oven:**
   - Place the skillet with the seared steaks in the preheated oven.
   - Bake for 5–8 minutes for medium-rare (or adjust cooking time for your desired doneness).
6. **Add Butter Finish:**
   - Remove the steaks from the oven. Add a pat of butter to the top of each steak and let it melt.
   - Rest the steaks for 5 minutes to allow juices to redistribute.
7. **Serve:**
   - Remove the toothpicks and serve immediately. Enjoy with your choice of side dishes!

Tips:

- Use a meat thermometer to check doneness (125°F for medium-rare, 135°F for medium).
- Pair with mashed potatoes, grilled vegetables, or a red wine sauce for an elevated meal!

Maple-Glazed Bacon Donuts

Ingredients:

- 2 cups all-purpose flour
- 2 teaspoons baking powder
- 1/2 teaspoon salt
- 1/2 cup sugar
- 3/4 cup milk
- 2 large eggs
- 1/4 cup unsalted butter, melted
- 1 teaspoon vanilla extract
- 6 slices bacon, cooked and crumbled

For the Maple Glaze:

- 1/4 cup maple syrup
- 1 cup powdered sugar
- 1 tablespoon milk

Instructions:

1. Preheat oven to 375°F (190°C) and grease a donut pan.
2. In a bowl, whisk together the flour, baking powder, salt, and sugar.
3. In another bowl, combine milk, eggs, melted butter, and vanilla.
4. Gradually mix wet ingredients into the dry ingredients until just combined.
5. Stir in half of the crumbled bacon.
6. Spoon the batter into the donut pan and bake for 10-12 minutes.
7. While cooling, make the glaze by whisking maple syrup, powdered sugar, and milk.
8. Dip donuts in the glaze and sprinkle with the remaining crumbled bacon.

Bacon-Wrapped Scallops

Ingredients:

- 12 large sea scallops
- 12 slices bacon
- 2 tablespoons olive oil
- Salt and pepper to taste
- Lemon wedges for serving

Instructions:

1. Preheat the oven to 425°F (220°C).
2. Pat scallops dry with paper towels and season with salt and pepper.
3. Wrap each scallop with a slice of bacon, securing with a toothpick.
4. Heat olive oil in a skillet over medium heat and sear each side of the scallops for 1 minute.
5. Transfer to a baking sheet and bake for 8-10 minutes until the bacon is crispy.
6. Serve hot with lemon wedges.

Candied Bacon Skewers

Ingredients:

- 12 slices thick-cut bacon
- 1/4 cup brown sugar
- 1/4 teaspoon cayenne pepper (optional)
- Wooden skewers

Instructions:

1. Preheat the oven to 350°F (175°C) and line a baking sheet with foil.
2. Mix brown sugar and cayenne pepper (if using) in a small bowl.
3. Thread each slice of bacon onto a skewer in a wavy pattern.
4. Coat the bacon with the sugar mixture.
5. Place the skewers on the baking sheet and bake for 25-30 minutes until caramelized and crispy.
6. Cool slightly before serving. Enjoy as a sweet and savory appetizer!

Bacon Jam Bruschetta

Ingredients:

- 1 baguette, sliced
- 1/2 cup bacon jam
- 1/4 cup goat cheese
- 2 tablespoons olive oil
- Fresh thyme for garnish

Instructions:

1. Preheat the oven to 375°F (190°C).
2. Brush baguette slices with olive oil and toast for 5-7 minutes.
3. Spread goat cheese on each slice, top with bacon jam, and garnish with thyme.

Chocolate-Dipped Bacon

Ingredients:

- 8 slices cooked bacon
- 1 cup dark chocolate chips
- Sea salt for garnish

Instructions:

1. Melt chocolate in a microwave or double boiler.
2. Dip half of each bacon slice in chocolate and lay on parchment paper.
3. Sprinkle with sea salt and chill until the chocolate sets.

Bacon and Cheddar Stuffed Mushrooms

Ingredients:

- 16 large mushrooms, stems removed
- 6 slices bacon, cooked and crumbled
- 1/2 cup shredded cheddar
- 1/4 cup cream cheese
- 2 tablespoons parsley, chopped

Instructions:

1. Preheat oven to 375°F (190°C).
2. Mix bacon, cheddar, cream cheese, and parsley.
3. Fill mushrooms with the mixture and bake for 15-20 minutes.

Bacon-Wrapped Asparagus Bundles

Ingredients:

- 1 bunch asparagus
- 6 slices bacon
- 1 tablespoon olive oil
- Salt and pepper to taste

Instructions:

1. Preheat oven to 400°F (200°C).
2. Bundle 3-4 asparagus stalks with a slice of bacon.
3. Drizzle with olive oil, season, and bake for 20-25 minutes.

Bacon-Wrapped Chicken Bites

Ingredients:

- 2 chicken breasts, cubed
- 12 slices bacon, halved
- 1/4 cup barbecue sauce
- Toothpicks

Instructions:

1. Preheat oven to 400°F (200°C).
2. Wrap each chicken cube with bacon and secure with a toothpick.
3. Brush with barbecue sauce and bake for 15-20 minutes.

Avocado Bacon Breakfast Toast

Ingredients:

- 4 slices of bread, toasted
- 2 avocados, mashed
- 8 slices bacon, cooked
- Salt, pepper, and chili flakes to taste

Instructions:

1. Spread mashed avocado on toast.
2. Top each slice with two pieces of bacon.
3. Season with salt, pepper, and chili flakes.

Bacon-Wrapped Pork Tenderloin

Ingredients:

- 1 pork tenderloin
- 8-10 slices bacon
- 2 tablespoons olive oil
- 1 teaspoon garlic powder
- 1/2 teaspoon paprika

Instructions:

1. Preheat oven to 375°F (190°C).
2. Season tenderloin with garlic powder and paprika.
3. Wrap with bacon and secure with toothpicks.
4. Bake for 25-30 minutes or until internal temp reaches 145°F (63°C).

Bacon Mac and Cheese

Ingredients:

- 8 oz elbow macaroni
- 4 cups shredded cheddar
- 4 slices bacon, cooked and crumbled
- 2 tablespoons butter
- 2 tablespoons flour
- 2 cups milk

Instructions:

1. Cook macaroni according to package instructions.
2. In a saucepan, melt butter, whisk in flour, and cook for 1 minute.
3. Gradually add milk, stirring until thickened.
4. Add cheese and stir until melted.
5. Mix in cooked pasta and top with crumbled bacon.

Bacon-Wrapped Jalapeño Poppers

Ingredients:

- 12 jalapeños, halved and seeded
- 8 oz cream cheese, softened
- 1/2 cup shredded cheddar cheese
- 12 slices bacon, halved
- Toothpicks

Instructions:

1. Preheat oven to 400°F (200°C).
2. Mix cream cheese and cheddar, then fill each jalapeño half.
3. Wrap with bacon and secure with toothpicks.
4. Bake for 20-25 minutes until bacon is crispy.

Bacon-Wrapped Shrimp

Ingredients:

- 16 large shrimp, peeled and deveined
- 8 slices bacon, halved
- 2 tablespoons olive oil
- 1/2 teaspoon smoked paprika
- Toothpicks

Instructions:

1. Preheat oven to 425°F (220°C).
2. Wrap each shrimp with bacon and secure with toothpicks.
3. Brush with olive oil and sprinkle with paprika.
4. Bake for 10-12 minutes.

Bacon and Egg Breakfast Pizza

Ingredients:

- 1 pizza dough
- 1/2 cup shredded mozzarella
- 4 eggs
- 6 slices bacon, cooked and crumbled
- 1/4 cup chopped green onions

Instructions:

1. Preheat oven to 450°F (230°C).
2. Roll out dough and top with mozzarella, bacon, and eggs.
3. Bake for 12-15 minutes.
4. Sprinkle with green onions before serving.

BLT Pasta Salad

Ingredients:

- 8 oz pasta, cooked and cooled
- 8 slices bacon, crumbled
- 1 cup cherry tomatoes, halved
- 1/2 cup mayonnaise
- 1/4 cup sour cream
- 2 cups lettuce, chopped

Instructions:

1. Mix mayonnaise and sour cream in a large bowl.
2. Toss in pasta, bacon, tomatoes, and lettuce.
3. Serve chilled.

Bacon Cheeseburger Sliders

Ingredients:

- 1 lb ground beef
- 8 slider buns
- 8 slices cheddar cheese
- 8 slices bacon, halved
- Lettuce, tomatoes, and pickles for topping

Instructions:

1. Form beef into small patties and cook in a skillet.
2. Place cheese on patties and let it melt.
3. Assemble sliders with bacon, lettuce, tomato, and pickles.

Bacon-Wrapped Meatloaf

Ingredients:

- 2 lbs ground beef
- 1 cup breadcrumbs
- 2 eggs
- 1/2 cup ketchup
- 1 onion, diced
- 8-10 slices bacon

Instructions:

1. Preheat oven to 375°F (190°C).
2. Mix beef, breadcrumbs, eggs, ketchup, and onions.
3. Shape into a loaf and wrap with bacon.
4. Bake for 50-60 minutes.

Bacon-Wrapped Dates with Goat Cheese

Ingredients:

- 12 dates, pitted
- 4 oz goat cheese
- 6 slices bacon, halved
- Toothpicks

Instructions:

1. Stuff each date with goat cheese.
2. Wrap with bacon and secure with toothpicks.
3. Bake at 400°F (200°C) for 10-12 minutes.

Cheddar Bacon Biscuits

Ingredients:

- 2 cups all-purpose flour
- 1 tablespoon baking powder
- 1/2 teaspoon salt
- 1/4 cup cold butter, cubed
- 1/2 cup shredded cheddar
- 6 slices bacon, crumbled
- 3/4 cup milk

Instructions:

1. Preheat oven to 425°F (220°C).
2. Mix flour, baking powder, and salt.
3. Cut in butter, then stir in cheddar, bacon, and milk.
4. Drop spoonfuls onto a baking sheet and bake for 12-15 minutes.

Bacon-Wrapped Salmon Fillet

Ingredients:

- 4 salmon fillets
- 8 slices bacon
- 2 tablespoons olive oil
- 1 teaspoon lemon zest

- Salt and pepper to taste

Instructions:

1. Preheat oven to 400°F (200°C).
2. Season salmon with salt, pepper, and lemon zest.
3. Wrap each fillet with 2 slices of bacon.
4. Heat olive oil in a skillet and sear fillets for 1 minute on each side.
5. Transfer to a baking sheet and bake for 10-12 minutes.

Brussels Sprouts with Bacon and Garlic

Ingredients:

- 1 lb Brussels sprouts, halved
- 6 slices bacon, chopped
- 3 garlic cloves, minced
- 2 tablespoons olive oil
- Salt and pepper to taste

Instructions:

1. Cook bacon in a skillet until crispy; remove and set aside.
2. Add garlic to the skillet and sauté for 1 minute.
3. Add Brussels sprouts, season, and sauté for 8-10 minutes.
4. Toss with crispy bacon before serving.

Bacon-Wrapped Cheese Sticks

Ingredients:

- 8 mozzarella sticks
- 8 slices bacon
- Toothpicks

Instructions:

1. Preheat oven to 400°F (200°C).
2. Wrap each mozzarella stick with bacon and secure with toothpicks.
3. Bake for 10-12 minutes until bacon is crispy.

Sweet and Spicy Bacon Crackers

Ingredients:

- 24 buttery crackers
- 12 slices bacon, halved
- 1/4 cup brown sugar
- 1/4 teaspoon cayenne pepper

Instructions:

1. Preheat oven to 350°F (175°C).
2. Place crackers on a baking sheet and top each with half a bacon slice.
3. Sprinkle with brown sugar and cayenne.
4. Bake for 20-25 minutes.

Carbonara with Crispy Bacon

Ingredients:

- 8 oz spaghetti
- 6 slices bacon, chopped
- 3 egg yolks
- 1/2 cup grated Parmesan
- 2 garlic cloves, minced
- Salt and pepper to taste

Instructions:

1. Cook pasta according to package instructions.
2. In a skillet, cook bacon until crispy; set aside.
3. Sauté garlic in the bacon fat for 1 minute.
4. Whisk egg yolks and Parmesan together.
5. Toss pasta with garlic, bacon, and egg mixture.

Bacon-Wrapped Hot Dogs

Ingredients:

- 8 hot dogs
- 8 slices bacon
- 8 hot dog buns
- Ketchup, mustard, and toppings of choice

Instructions:

1. Preheat oven to 400°F (200°C).
2. Wrap each hot dog with bacon and secure with toothpicks.
3. Bake for 12-15 minutes.
4. Serve in buns with your favorite toppings.

Bacon and Mushroom Risotto

Ingredients:

- 1 1/2 cups Arborio rice
- 6 slices bacon, chopped
- 8 oz mushrooms, sliced
- 1/2 cup Parmesan cheese

- 4 cups chicken broth, warmed
- 1 onion, diced

Instructions:

1. Cook bacon until crispy; remove and set aside.
2. Sauté onion and mushrooms in bacon fat.
3. Add rice and stir for 2 minutes.
4. Gradually add broth, stirring until absorbed.
5. Stir in Parmesan and bacon before serving.

Bacon and Potato Frittata

Ingredients:

- 6 eggs
- 4 slices bacon, cooked and crumbled
- 2 potatoes, thinly sliced
- 1/2 cup shredded cheese

- 1/4 cup milk
- Salt and pepper to taste

Instructions:

1. Preheat oven to 375°F (190°C).
2. In a skillet, cook potatoes until tender.
3. Whisk eggs, milk, salt, and pepper together.
4. Pour egg mixture over potatoes and top with bacon and cheese.
5. Bake for 15-20 minutes until set.

Bacon-Wrapped Pineapple Bites

Ingredients:

- 24 pineapple chunks
- 12 slices bacon, halved
- 1/4 cup brown sugar
- Toothpicks

Instructions:

1. Preheat oven to 400°F (200°C).
2. Wrap each pineapple chunk with bacon and secure with a toothpick.
3. Sprinkle with brown sugar.
4. Bake for 15-20 minutes until bacon is crispy.

Bacon-Wrapped Corn on the Cob

Ingredients:

- 4 ears of corn, husked
- 8 slices bacon
- 2 tablespoons butter, melted
- Salt and pepper to taste

Instructions:

1. Preheat grill to medium heat.
2. Wrap each ear of corn with 2 slices of bacon.
3. Brush with melted butter and season with salt and pepper.
4. Grill for 15-20 minutes, rotating often.

Bacon-Wrapped Onion Rings

Ingredients:

- 2 large onions, sliced into rings
- 12 slices bacon
- 1/2 cup barbecue sauce

Instructions:

1. Preheat oven to 375°F (190°C).
2. Wrap bacon around each onion ring.
3. Brush with barbecue sauce.
4. Bake for 20-25 minutes until crispy.

Bacon-Stuffed Chicken Breast

Ingredients:

- 4 chicken breasts
- 6 slices bacon, cooked and crumbled
- 1/2 cup shredded mozzarella
- 2 tablespoons cream cheese

- Salt and pepper to taste

Instructions:

1. Preheat oven to 375°F (190°C).
2. Cut a slit in each chicken breast and stuff with bacon, mozzarella, and cream cheese.
3. Season with salt and pepper.
4. Bake for 25-30 minutes.

Bacon Pancakes with Syrup

Ingredients:

- 1 1/2 cups pancake mix
- 6 slices bacon, cooked and crumbled
- 1 egg

- 1 cup milk
- Maple syrup for serving

Instructions:

1. Prepare pancake batter by mixing pancake mix, egg, and milk.
2. Stir in crumbled bacon.
3. Cook pancakes on a griddle until golden brown.
4. Serve with maple syrup.

Bacon-Wrapped Sausage Links

Ingredients:

- 12 breakfast sausage links
- 12 slices bacon
- Toothpicks

Instructions:

1. Preheat oven to 400°F (200°C).
2. Wrap each sausage link with a slice of bacon.
3. Secure with a toothpick and bake for 15-18 minutes.

Bacon and Spinach Quiche

Ingredients:

- 1 pie crust
- 6 slices bacon, cooked and crumbled
- 2 cups fresh spinach

- 1 cup shredded cheese
- 4 eggs
- 1/2 cup milk
- Salt and pepper to taste

Instructions:

1. Preheat oven to 350°F (175°C).
2. Place spinach and bacon in the pie crust.
3. Whisk eggs, milk, salt, and pepper, then pour over fillings.
4. Bake for 30-35 minutes until set.

Grilled Bacon-Wrapped Peaches

Ingredients:

- 4 peaches, halved and pitted
- 8 slices bacon
- 2 tablespoons honey

- Toothpicks

Instructions:

1. Preheat grill to medium heat.
2. Wrap each peach half with a slice of bacon and secure with toothpicks.
3. Grill for 8-10 minutes, brushing with honey halfway through.

Bacon Caesar Salad

Ingredients:

- 6 cups romaine lettuce, chopped
- 6 slices bacon, cooked and crumbled
- 1/2 cup Caesar dressing

- 1/4 cup grated Parmesan cheese
- Croutons for topping

Instructions:

1. In a large bowl, combine romaine lettuce, crumbled bacon, and Caesar dressing.
2. Toss until well coated.
3. Top with Parmesan cheese and croutons before serving.

Bacon and Cheddar Deviled Eggs

Ingredients:

- 6 hard-boiled eggs, halved
- 3 slices bacon, cooked and crumbled

- 1/4 cup mayonnaise
- 1/4 cup shredded cheddar cheese
- Salt and pepper to taste

Instructions:

1. Remove yolks from egg halves and place in a bowl.
2. Mash yolks with mayonnaise, bacon, cheddar, salt, and pepper.
3. Spoon or pipe mixture back into egg whites.

Bacon-Wrapped Meatballs

Ingredients:

- 1 lb ground beef

- 8 slices bacon, halved
- 1/2 cup breadcrumbs
- 1/4 cup grated Parmesan cheese
- 1 egg
- Salt and pepper to taste

Instructions:

1. Preheat oven to 375°F (190°C).
2. In a bowl, combine ground beef, breadcrumbs, Parmesan, egg, salt, and pepper.
3. Form into meatballs and wrap each with a half slice of bacon.
4. Bake for 20-25 minutes until cooked through.

Bacon-Wrapped Mozzarella Sticks

Ingredients:

- 12 mozzarella sticks
- 12 slices bacon
- Toothpicks

Instructions:

1. Preheat oven to 400°F (200°C).
2. Wrap each mozzarella stick with bacon and secure with a toothpick.
3. Bake for 10-12 minutes until bacon is crispy.

Maple-Bacon Ice Cream

Ingredients:

- 2 cups heavy cream
- 1 cup whole milk
- 1/2 cup maple syrup
- 6 slices bacon, cooked and crumbled
- 1 teaspoon vanilla extract

Instructions:

1. In a bowl, whisk together cream, milk, maple syrup, and vanilla.
2. Stir in crumbled bacon.
3. Pour mixture into an ice cream maker and churn according to manufacturer instructions.

Bacon and Brie Grilled Cheese

Ingredients:

- 4 slices bread
- 4 slices brie cheese
- 4 slices bacon, cooked
- 2 tablespoons butter

Instructions:

1. Butter one side of each slice of bread.
2. Place brie and bacon between two slices of bread, buttered sides out.
3. Grill on medium heat until golden brown on both sides and cheese is melted.

Bacon-Wrapped Avocado Fries

Ingredients:

- 2 ripe avocados, sliced into wedges
- 8 slices bacon
- Salt and pepper to taste

Instructions:

1. Preheat oven to 400°F (200°C).
2. Wrap each avocado wedge with a slice of bacon.
3. Place on a baking sheet and season with salt and pepper.
4. Bake for 15-20 minutes until bacon is crispy.

Bacon Cornbread Muffins

Ingredients:

- 1 cup cornmeal
- 1 cup all-purpose flour
- 1/4 cup sugar
- 1 tablespoon baking powder
- 1/2 teaspoon salt
- 1 cup milk
- 1/3 cup vegetable oil
- 2 eggs
- 6 slices bacon, cooked and crumbled

Instructions:

1. Preheat oven to 400°F (200°C).
2. In a bowl, combine cornmeal, flour, sugar, baking powder, and salt.
3. In another bowl, whisk together milk, oil, and eggs.
4. Combine wet and dry ingredients and fold in crumbled bacon.
5. Pour into muffin tins and bake for 15-20 minutes.

Sweet Chili Bacon Wings

Ingredients:

- 2 lbs chicken wings
- 6 slices bacon, chopped
- 1/2 cup sweet chili sauce
- 1 tablespoon soy sauce
- 1 tablespoon lime juice
- Salt and pepper to taste

Instructions:

1. Preheat oven to 400°F (200°C).
2. In a bowl, mix sweet chili sauce, soy sauce, lime juice, salt, and pepper.
3. Toss chicken wings in the sauce mixture.
4. Arrange wings on a baking sheet and sprinkle with chopped bacon.
5. Bake for 30-35 minutes until wings are crispy.

Lobster with Bacon Butter

Ingredients:

- 2 lobster tails
- 4 slices bacon, chopped
- 1/4 cup unsalted butter, softened
- 2 tablespoons fresh parsley, chopped
- Salt and pepper to taste

Instructions:

1. Preheat oven to 375°F (190°C).
2. Cook chopped bacon in a skillet until crispy, then drain on paper towels.
3. In a bowl, mix butter with bacon, parsley, salt, and pepper.
4. Split lobster tails and brush with bacon butter.
5. Bake for 15-20 minutes until lobster is cooked through.

Bacon-Stuffed French Toast

Ingredients:

- 8 slices bread
- 4 slices bacon, cooked and crumbled
- 4 oz cream cheese, softened
- 4 eggs
- 1 cup milk
- 1 teaspoon vanilla extract
- Maple syrup for serving

Instructions:

1. In a bowl, mix cream cheese and crumbled bacon.
2. Spread the mixture between two slices of bread to make a sandwich.
3. In another bowl, whisk eggs, milk, and vanilla.
4. Dip sandwiches in the egg mixture and cook on a skillet until golden brown.
5. Serve with maple syrup.

Bacon-Wrapped Water Chestnuts

Ingredients:

- 12 water chestnuts, peeled
- 6 slices bacon, cut in half
- 1/4 cup soy sauce
- 1 tablespoon brown sugar

Instructions:

1. Preheat oven to 375°F (190°C).
2. Wrap each water chestnut with a half slice of bacon and secure with a toothpick.
3. In a bowl, mix soy sauce and brown sugar, then brush over wrapped water chestnuts.
4. Bake for 25-30 minutes until bacon is crispy.

Bacon and Apple Grilled Sandwich

Ingredients:

- 4 slices bread
- 4 slices bacon, cooked
- 1 apple, thinly sliced
- 4 slices cheddar cheese
- 2 tablespoons butter

Instructions:

1. Butter one side of each slice of bread.
2. Layer bacon, apple slices, and cheese between two slices of bread, buttered side out.
3. Grill on medium heat until golden brown and cheese is melted.

Bacon-Wrapped Turkey Breast

Ingredients:

- 1 boneless turkey breast (about 2 lbs)
- 10 slices bacon
- 1 tablespoon olive oil
- Salt and pepper to taste
- Fresh herbs (thyme or rosemary) for seasoning

Instructions:

1. Preheat oven to 375°F (190°C).
2. Season turkey breast with salt, pepper, and herbs.
3. Wrap bacon around the turkey breast, securing with toothpicks if necessary.
4. Heat olive oil in a skillet and sear the wrapped turkey for 2-3 minutes on each side.
5. Transfer to the oven and bake for 25-30 minutes until cooked through.